A 8
w

# Quiet Book

—

Pattie McCarthy

*Apogee Press*
*Berkeley · California*
*2016*

## Acknowledgements

Pages / poems in these series first appeared in the following publications : Academy of American Poets Poem-a-Day, ed. Alex Dimitrov; *Bloof Books Sampler*, ed. Shanna Compton; *Boog City*, ed. Buck Downs; *Cleaver Magazine*, ed. Karen Rile; *Dusie Tuesday Poems*, ed. Rob McLennan & Susana Gardner; *Horse Less Review*, ed. Jen Tynes, Erika Howsare, Jennifer Denrow, & Michael Sikkema; *Omniverse*, ed. Rusty Morrison & Ken Keegan; *N/A*, ed. françois luong & Amish Trivedi; *your impossible voice*, ed. Karen Biscopink; *Z"L*, ed. Ash Smith.

Thank you to the editors for your hard work & support.

*x y z &&* first appeared as a chapbook from Ahsahta Press. Thank you especially to Janet Holmes.

Fifteen pages from 'genre scenes' appeared as *fifteen genre scenes*, a handwritten scribal-experiment chapbook from eth press. Thank you so much to David Hadbawnik & Chris Piuma.

The poem "notes for clothespin" was commissioned for *Sound Sculptures*, a series of sonic responses to various sculptures commissioned by the Philadelphia Redevelopment Authority's Percent for Art program. *Sound Sculptures* was commissioned by the Philadelphia Redevelopment Authority and was curated and produced by Bowerbird. Thank you to Chris Forsyth for this opportunity.

Book design: Philip Krayna, Conifer Creative
www.conifercreative.com

Cover painting: *Night Kitchen* by Kate Kern Mundie, used with permission of the artist.
www.katekernmundie.com

ISBN 978-0-9851007-6-6
Library of Congress Card Number 2014953656

Published by Apogee Press, 2308 Sixth Street, Berkeley, CA, 94710.
www.apogeepress.com

# Table of Contents

Mammal messages able to evolve privately between beings.
—Joseph McElroy, "Night Soul"

# x y z & &

a crown for her head with
castles upon it, skyscrapers
filled with nut-chocolates—
—William Carlos Williams, *Spring & All*


Sending his mother to the typewriter
To type a poem that would embarrass him
Years later
—Anselm Berrigan, "Looking through a slant of light"

& to & such a pretty bird. this is
the first sonnet for the third baby. if
I sound prepared for that, I am not.
let me know you're all right in there, would you?
Kevin says : I dreamt it was a boy.
my brother says : your favorite presidents
cannot be FDR & Jefferson—
that's illogical. Emmett says : when I
was pregnant with you, that was a tough week too.
Asher says : seashell, voilà.          & the third
(having outgrown a perfect, fragile world)
baby     (*bird* from *brid* OE from unknown
origin)                    "because he was crying
I like him most of all," says my son.

a couple of breaks of sunshine over
the next couple hours, what little sun
shine there is left. a view that outranks
me : two baseball fields, two bridges, the dome
(golden) of a church I can't identify.
a ludicrous little halo.                a noun
formal or technical.        moxibustion
vertex    frank    footling    complete. (she turns) she
turns (she turned) her own version.        like ploughing
a field    like a furrow        like verse or        versus
(preposition)    against or toward        furrow
like a harrow (what a harrow is for)
verso    (on the turned)   like the turn in a sonnet.
sleep with arms around my children, as if—

when she wakes from her nap, she knows all her
sins can't be forgiven. I asked him what
he was made of & he replied : Asher
made of Far Rockaway            (see toponymy of New Netherland).
milk fever             the *te deum* of the nursery
(this little motion) did you notice any
profound motion?        the last one, the third
baby—   I thought I'd remember the delivery
details better             (surrender someone or some
thing)— Middle English from Old French, based on
Latin *de-* 'away' plus *liberare* 'set free' (see :
how it makes sense that the midwife asked you :
do you want to set her free? offering
you the cord for cutting.)        hold her unutterable

(2/23/11)

1.20 a.m. that smart sallowlass just hopped

1.40 a.m. she doesn't even have her own bed. she instead sleeps warm & sweet,
swaddled, between.

3.30 a.m. the open mouth        the small O & so specific.

4.40 a.m. wet slate of her eyes    open    done nursing    eyes open    (please go back to sleep).

7.15 a.m. three children & a dog, noisy at breakfast. carry me carry me, the heavy boys say.

8.30 a.m. the day she was born, my body felt intrusive & huge. incidentally, it still does.

10.30 a.m. the midwife's discharge instructions included : no stairs & do not carry heavy
boys for two weeks.

11.15 a.m. I am certain I was screaming                but he tells me I was apologizing.

1.00 p.m. such a pretty bird.

2.20 p.m. such a pretty house & such a pretty garden.

4.50 p.m. milk fever        cluster  to nurse & be nursed. warm & sweet, small & swaddled.
& so specific.

7.00 p.m. postpartum chills        postpartum bleeding        post-

9.00 - 10.30 p.m. cluster feeding.

11.50 p.m. Saint Beauty is a girl from elementary school.

witching hour detente          cluster feeding
co-sleeping cluster nursing witching hour
mirror neurons          witching hour colic
derivatives      colicky          adjective
witching hour          colic    cluster detente
a colicky disorder to which she
                         is too subject witching cluster co-
sleeping        & so fetching    a pretty bird
*hex*    first a verb in Pennsylvania Dutch
          in a c.1250 translation of Exodus, *witches* is used of the Egyptian
          midwives who save the newborn sons of the Hebrews
colic          hour detente    little nursling
a witch has been known to cry out while her husband
places inside her the image of a child.

her suggestion of sheep      fragmented sleep
such a pretty girl such a pretty girl
something soothing to the eyes like treetops
clergybirds in formation, form in sun—
cowbird, clergybird, chickadee, acorns.
can't sew a hole, my mother always says.
all edges      rattling in my corner.
I wrote that line down & I've already
forgotten it      as much as possible
I wear the baby & fill my head with
Asher's toddler chatter. it evens me
out. something soothing to the eyes like sleep.
already I miss having you always with me.
I'm beginning to find my head again.

blank blank blank blank blank blank blank blank blank blank
blank blank blank blank blank blank blank blank blank blank
blank blank blank blank blank blank blank blank blank blank
blank blank blank blank blank blank blank blank blank blank
blank blank blank blank blank blank blank blank blank blank
blank blank blank blank blank blank blank blank blank blank
blank blank blank blank blank blank blank blank blank blank
blank blank blank blank blank blank blank blank blank blank
blank blank blank blank blank blank blank blank blank blank
blank blank blank blank blank blank blank blank blank blank
blank blank blank blank blank blank blank blank blank blank
babywearing, assures the Mobywrap ad,
reduces crying significantly.
there's nothing wrong with me. I feel fine.

nursing in an uncomfortable chair
nursing in a hostile pizzeria
nursing in an Anthropologie dressing room
nursing in public nursing in public
nursing in an empty church (OLG)*
nursing in the Babies R Us 'mother's room'
nursing in the Ikea 'family room'
nursing in our bed nursing in our bed
nursing in the Honda Odyssey
nursing in front of my father-in-law
nursing in optimism, book in hand
nursing in a history of privacy
nursing in a crowd on the boardwalk
nursing in Rittenhouse Square, a picnic


*Our Lady of Guadalupe

milk fever cluster feeding witching hour
cluster feeding milk fever witching hour
witching hour milk fever cluster feeding
witching hour cluster feeding milk fever.
postpartum chills postpartum bleeding post-
partum chills postpartum bleeding post part-
the part after parting          but it's not—
it's *the* part. that part is the whole. to part
is the whole part. when I was in labor
he said : she's coming like a cannonball
on a bobsled. I said I wasn't ready
& the midwife said : well, she's here. she's blonde.
I mean that a thing who seems
continuous is made up of two parts.

a bird cows were stirred a third. a third is all.
a ludicrous little halo. & up
in the nursery an absurd little bird—
already I miss having you always
with me. something easy on the eyes like
the spines of books— have you a daughter?
while she is mine (I'm learning her language)—
a steep coast, a brae (crashing in her eye
lashes) in the tenth magnitude— (see listen)
see. (see a butterfly)      with wings that vary
see history too  (with wings that vary)
I'm learning her language (while she is mine)
hold her unutterable— in girls' rooms
(pretty bird) some bird brought you here on foot

aren't children little pears & observant
birds. dear Fionnuala & your two little
sharp teeth : what's great about the quiet car :
the businessmen read the paper on paper.
I'm wearing wellies & wellie-warmers
I'll spend almost $8 on coffee
                    while at work—
                                (I miss the baby)
in physics, a *daughter* is a nuclide
formed by the radioactive decay
of another. of course, *mother* rhymes with
*another*. but this is just too meta-
& silly & loaded for me. pinion
on the clean fin clear clear wave          always at a loss,
we remain open, persons in process.

turtle into it with your little force.
dear Fionnuala & your three little teeth :
the 3:10 never happens at 3:10—
but I am on my way, heavy, to you.
*Fionnuala* is not in the top 1000
female names for any year of birth
in the last one-hundred-thirty-one years.
please enter another name.
nursing in the Philadelphia
Museum of Art cafeteria annex
nursing in a seaside-colored rocker
some bird brought you here in her eyelashes.
I have three babies tonight, all three are
sleeping [. . .] heavy breathing baby bodies

my first winter Paris hat. I still have it.
nursing in the quiet car   R5        outbound
overbrook next overbrook overbrook
it looks like Fionnuala is counting
syllables on her fingers in her sleep.
I watch the sky move in three squares of bay
window, the lower halves shuttered to different
degrees by more-or-less working louvers.
wynnewood next wynnewood ardmore next ardmore
& then a mile walk in the early
dark & rain. nursing in a quiet room.
an absurd little bird brought you here on foot.
your four little teeth & a perfect automobile going thirty
miles an hour on a smooth road to a twelfth-century cathedral.

the Comcast building sponsors the sky, dear
Fionnuala, divide history into
convenient chunks, easier to carry
& easier to essay— to 1066
before 1789        after
1789        to 1865
after 1865        since 1922
before 1845 & after
                    1852        before & after
ante- & post-    & in parting
parture        (like departure & in partu)
is obsolete, is both noun & action—
long ago, when daughter & laughter rhymed—
daughter is an edge, edge a verb—

both nuns & mothers worship images.
under a spire at the piano.
thistles, birds' nests to the left of the church.
boys build a ringfort & say *carry me*.
I ordered in the Starbucks demotic.
he mows the lawn into a labyrinth.
he mows the lawn into a striped outfield.

      see also : hexenmilch    each of us carries
around a set of shibboleths with totemic
reverence meanwhile    we trample blithely on spells
                & hexes we have never heard of
a rückenfigur, himself, the two boys
triangulate, after dinner baseball—
children playing against mud, against sand

next summer I will build my box all over
again      next summer I'd like a big plate
of oysters & the harshest   cheapest grappa
you got        next summer if it's next summer
then I love you      next next summer little
warm body little ice cream breath if next
summer          then I'm sleeping in next summer
next summer the sky is divided into windows      (see
listen) see unutterable      next summer
I'll have some decaf next summer potatoes
au gratin & mashed next summer      potatoes
two ways next   summer is both noun & action
next summer little boys their sticky feet
next summer or I fly my rounds      tempestuous

but this slow, too-dark softness of the light-coming-into-things reminds me of London mornings, when you wake up & go straight out to get *The Guardian* for your dad. I make a little mime of snowballs— hands cupped & rounded & they turn into my dad's hands. it's startling & I'm startled. I keep doing it, keep repeating the gesture, want the image to happen again but it doesn't.     dormez-vous     dormez-vous     Asher sings in his sweet sing-song toddler voice. we should record it.     arc de nothing     he says when tired of exhibiting. when will you be old enough to send alone to the newsagents for matches & *The Times*? one evening, driving home from piano, a man who looked so like him crossed the street (jaywalked) right in front of our car & he was carrying an *Inquirer* & a coffee, wearing running shorts in winter. I made a sound. Emmett asked what happened. O wonderful son, that can so astonish a mother. O lord thou pluckest me out. O lord thou pluckest (Augustine qtd. in Eliot qtd. in McCarthy).

he's seeing something I will never see.
[repeat for a total of fourteen lines]

*espresso in utero* : Fionnuala's
Latin motto.     no subject offers
a greater opportunity for terrible
writing than motherhood.      I'm re-broody
          (the verb lit. *to hatch by heat*) & that which
has gravity but no light today.
the gull is my favorite of the fake
birds (I knew it was not a gull).
a couple of breaks of sunshine over
              unutterable      indivisible.
I had four hours in a row alone
to work & I looked at photos of them
& remembered the limitless mistakes
it was possible to make with the piano.

the Comcast building sponsors the sky, omelette
dear, rattle at it, rattle your little
fierce. next summer you'll be in sand, in dirt,
in play— this summer in a small, unfragile
round— taking on your shape, filling your shape.
both noun & action— like the turn in
a sonnet. & up in the nursery
          an absurd        a pretty              & such a bird
(how did you get here?)   pretty rattle fierce.
omelette            unutterable    the sky &
the open mouth     the small *O* & so
specific. you will smell very sweet— you
will remember a private sea. I want
a nice little boat made out of ocean.

the infant whispered like thought, old things are what
[she] whispered into his thinking.          summer
as noun & action          I said your name again
an archdiocesan box lunch          & action
the current study examined the ability of whines,
cries, & motherese to distract listeners.
all participants completed a series of simple subtraction
problems while listening to these attachment
vocalizations as well as to machine noise, neutral speech, & silence.
          they laid you on my chest          I said your name
          the everyday opera          Fionnuala
at 3:00 a.m. the wind blew all the doors
closed inside the house & then it was fall.
he talks in maths & buzzes like a fridge.

failing to make it as a circle, one
can always become an angle.
   build it  disappear into it easy
the sky is a labyrinth of spells &
hexes we have never heard of the small
open mouth now  full of teeth oyster shells
nursing in you're *still* nursing overnight?
   I heard him say my name I heard myself
say I'm afraid & we were moving
the gurney in the hall saying push now
but I didn't want to give birth there
so I rolled onto my side & went quiet.
everything went white. like a wall it fell.
ashes & arms fall down all around me.

the cry of the gulls. the line between water
& grammar. Descartes' clockwork daughter sinks
& flutters, buzzes like a fridge & swims.
       attachment vocalizations
       machine noise   neutral speech &
       silence  silence  silence  silence
counting the moos & woofs & nods as words.
she stretches half the length of me, half-way
through the night. I think, rather, to learn her
language instead. & hexes we have
       never heard of—       I think, rather,
       to ignore them. I was here the whole time—
her brother says. yes, I think, & you all were —
saint beauty     saint sleep     saint sweet     saint syllable

this body is stolen first from the girl—
      chiefly in plural    a child of either
     sex      a young person now Irish English
European clothing names & the etym
                      ology of girl    suggests the reflex
the attested Old English word *gyrela*
                 dress     a quite different theory  Middle Low
German *Göre*        see English girl under
the asterisked sky of Indo-European
     herself as a modernity more stunning
moving through moving into super
               stitious & penitential spaces
a landscape with figure  (trans.) to provide with
a girl or girls    (cite)         as verbs in winter

in a serious storm of being aliveness teem,
I think, rather, to learn her language instead.
she takes the vowel from owl & wraps it around
my head.        I sit by her crib & say : stay
                with me please stay   hit all the milestones
on time      no need to be a genius or
                a beautifully behaved automaton :
one little robot two little robots three little robots
all in a row in the frigid preschool
                                parking lot. please be rowdy & know your
own mind.      please sing it's beautiful but screaming
hurts my head this morning. please put your coats
on please put your hats on sing        alphabet
alive beneath the alphabet so far

I dissolves to a haven of buzzing
(the voices of children, freshness of surprise)
*iconostasis* does not, it turns out,
mean 'an icon standing still' (well, not really,
& too bad, because I have long enjoyed
this private image of the icon's body
at rest).          a playground stoppage   an instance
a small stillness in the whirl & cold sounds
verbs in winter       unclockwork daughter.
on Thursday she said nouns all day        two days
later she said 'otters eat waffles' &
                        other magnificent sentences.
a child— pleased with the sound of my own
name repeating it over & over

an ounce is a unit of time equal to

one-twelfth of a moment        or seven & a half seconds

an ounce of time can be divided into forty-seven atoms

my father used to call me on the phone everyday      one day

he called to tell me that he would not

do chemo or radiation     &

never called me on the phone again        even though there were

two months more       he would talk in ounces

in the background & my mother would repeat his

words to me        thereafter      (a protractor        a full

set of world book encyclopedias & a shag rug

the color of what I thought                  'amber waves of grain'

must be)        it involves no breach of continuity & is but

a continuation of the vital processes going on     in the parental body.

the first birth in fourteen lines

line one. first contraction on the subway (Broad St line, northbound)
line two. taught two classes (honors intro to lit & contemporary innovative poetry by women)
line three. ate huge bowl of pasta at home (cavatelli with veggies)
line four. slept briefly
line five. woke to active labor at 11.30 pm (watched Daily Show, watched NYPD Blue)
line six. went through transition in the car
line seven. got a great parking spot on ninth street at Clinton around 1.30 a.m.
line eight. arrived at PETU dilated nine centimeters
line nine. posterior presentation, also known as sunny-side-up
line ten. turned the baby by assuming side-lying position on alternating sides with each contraction
line eleven. for approximately two hours, at which point the baby turned over-easy
line twelve. nuchal cord
line thirteen. total pushing from approximately 3.30 a.m. until 6.01 a.m., one and a half stitches
line fourteen. 22 inches long, 7 lbs., 13 oz.

the second birth in fourteen lines

line one. water broke at 10.30 p.m.
line two. as I was sitting down on the couch to watch House after making hot cocoa
line three. called Jenn McCreary, who lived one block away, to come stay with Emmett
line four. it was her birthday & she said she'd be over as soon as she put on some pants
line five. we packed a bag
line six. it started to snow as we drove to the hospital
line seven. got the same great parking spot on ninth street at Clinton around 11.30 p.m.
line eight. in PETU given a hep-lock instead of an IV upon request, arm ballooned
line nine. impatient Austrian midwife wanted to administer pitocin around midnight
line ten. requested & received an hour of wait & see; snow, snow, & snow
line eleven. first contraction at 12.30 a.m., fully dilated by 1.30 a.m.
line twelve. precipitous labor
line thirteen. total pushing from approximately 1.45 a.m. until 3.01 a.m., four stitches
line fourteen. 20 inches long, 7 lbs., 5 oz.

the third birth in fourteen lines

line one. bloody show in Karin McGrath Dunn's bathroom around 3.30 p.m.
line two. pushed double stroller home (three blocks) with two boys in it
line three. stopped for first contraction outside Ippolito's Seafood (13th & Dickinson)
line four. got pizza for dinner (Francoluigi's, 13th & Tasker)
line five. bedtime books with the boys, contractions ten minutes apart
line six. no sleep
line seven. got a decent parking spot on the 700 block of Spruce St. just after midnight
line eight. & arrived fully dilated
line nine. someone said ring of fire
line ten. which I didn't think was a thing people really said to women in labor
line eleven. I heard him say my name & I opened my mouth
line twelve. but I don't know what came out
line thirteen. total pushing from approximately 12.40 until 1.09 a.m., two stitches
line fourteen. 20 inches long, 7 lbs., 12 oz., eyes open

whirling their skirts about until they stand
out flat— they play at mass & house & scourge
('not a safe game')          & knucklebones & rock
paper scissors        they play at trucks & farm.
when the three children play Harry Potter
the girl gets to be Harry                  that's brother-love.
hexenmilch        (milch pleez        she says) this body.
they play at school        they play at basehit        they
play wug test.        two months weaned she still turns her
body as if to nurse when sleepy        she
still jams her hand down my shirt          because nursing
wasn't physically intimate enough
            she'd hook a finger in my ear & pull
            my face down to hers                  girl can be a verb

the blue of larkspur     the blur of larkspur
like wet wool like a rain soaked wool kilt drying
slowly over the course of the day by
occupying desks near warm radiators
until sixth or seventh period
                    (trigonometry? bio two?) a kind
of animal smell the damp hair
sticks to the back of her neck the fever
breaks & makes this snow smell like this smell not
unpleasant but not conventionally
pleasant like puppy breath it must have
                    an evolutionary purpose
like I love your morning breath I'll take
care of you forever     hold her unutterable

I believe in neither superman nor
virgin birth but I believe in you, Elżbieta
Jabłońska.          & though I spent over
four of the last six years nursing someone,
there are no photos of me doing so
            except this one awkward selfie when she
            was around eighteen months old & in it
            she's got the corner of her eye on the iphone.
maybe in some weird corner I do believe
in the virgin birth the way an older
kid believes in santa just to be safe.
alas, I could never be a good
Quaker.          self-immolation is a big
            girl word but everyone's wearing it.

notes for clothespin

suppose the clothespin     spring-
loaded for clouds        see

also & see
through

weathering         its backbends
bellies attractive          domestic
                                          practical &

monument         I want to walk
around & around & around it until
William Penn fits in its pinch

genre : common
artifacts & its significance (if
any) is unknown

the gaze of the clothespin
falls on itself

with or as
with the fingers
             myself awake

the kiss is domestic is
domestic is kiss monumental

breech upon which
so much pinch


             I think when they
say *architectural* they mean that    it's more
             serious than *domestic*

             in that they wish to return
             & he asks if only
             one of those lovers has arms
             if they are on their tiptoes
             making a kind of funnel for sky

suppose closed   suppose up-
                              ended
genre : common
fingers            thumb & pointer
                   democratized & the grasp
                   bicentennial &

the grasp
shifts from a clench to a pinch
          its function fixed


                              spring-
loaded   lovers               armed
                   & when the spring gets skewed


          weathering the liberties
          suppose

he says to the clothespin
                    get a room

a kind of funnel their
faces the sky in its mouth
intimacy on this scale just
before or just after but what
if the gaze of the clothespin falls on
                              myself awake

breech upon which
etymological twins     a pigeon
                  in the spring


           NO       loitering
                  soliciting
                  sitting or standing
                  skateboarding


lovers with or
as with the fingers
        false friends & when
                the spring
gets the grammar of together    see
also & walk
        around


the tension between domestic & public
around & around & around its
pinch between this & monument

# genre scenes

I'm building the haystack
I'll disappear into
   —Elizabeth Willis, "Unseasonable Pastoral"

a woman peeling apples, with a small child


straight off the blade she hands
it over her small hand the long peel for divination
the long peel hissing like a boa constrictor          how long
it must take to dress the daughter in all of her
gathers & kirtles & caps
her pinafore pockets full of oyster shells yes


what she can't see          what hurts her eyes          & like a genre painting I'll include

the image of another          painting or          a mirror
or a dog                    how Vermeer preferred women working alone
                    how this also   uses natural light in an otherwise unlit interior

when the old woman peels apples she's surrounded
by circles & keeps          her book in good light          & when
she is young it's a rich    brocade          steady hands
a hairband & a little jut of thought in her jaw                    (see also *dutch   quiet*   )

• Pieter de Hooch, *A Woman Peeling Apples, with a Small Child*, 1663
• Nicolaes Maes, *Old Woman Peeling Apples*, c. 1655
• Nicolaes Maes, *Young Woman Peeling Apples*, c. 1655

more about apples
        *for Kate Kern Mundie*


felix culpa
two apples        not
                  four hats rather

apples one
red one green one
leafed one stemmed one unstumped

they are not children's cheeks
or two dupas or nursing breasts or
raindrums or raindrums they resemble

themselves various yes   a stilleven
in lapsus        (we
                  don't eat the ones already on the ground)
themselves not knowledge but

apples   who
would take a naked
bareass baby to an orchard
I ask you that

where your hand has been I
sink & crisp my teeth

• Kate Kern Mundie, *Ripe Apples*, 2012

& child, with apples


when red & yellow leaves are on the trees the children
are not apples the children          chanting
          chapter one     in which     chapter two     in which
& heavy-lidded                what letter makes the *ah* sound
                              what letter makes the *puh* sound
                              what letter makes the *puh* sound
                              what letter makes the *la* sound
                              who can turn a can into a cane


after the great vowel shift       all word-final schwas were lost
when daughter & laughter rhymed       playground sounds in cold air
it coils off the table it spirals into her lap & under an enormous
hat her face is undeniably apple-shaped       one face &
hold this apple dear let me comb your hair


        • Gerard ter Borch, *Woman Peeling Apple*, 1650
        • Gerard ter Borch, *Woman Combing the Hair of Her Child*, 1653

woman nursing an infant with a child feeding a dog

the smell of blood & witch hazel
stuck in the throat like something
cold & the sugar smell of breastmilk &
the leftovers fed to the dog & the dog (like
apples) what women do with their hands
& the apple— or is it a small pumpkin— on the mantel
an exact echo in shape & size    apples
that were wintered over        & out the window
a distraction of seasonal color        a marriage nestorizing
the phonics trembling      the damp thing
*argle-bargled like an apple-wife*        what we are doing in warm lit rooms
her feet are up   liminal domestic texture without mirror      odd
daughter fodders      embers      & for the dog potato
& apple peels for long division                her cap tips back as she latches

• Pieter de Hooch, *Woman Nursing an Infant with a Child Feeding a Dog*, c. 1658-60

dear mary letter, with coda




since there is always
another one to be found—
        she uses the breast-over-bodice technique
        & some say she looks openly defiant but      she's wearing her title
        half-length  in a feigned oval      hammer price thirty-six
        thousand dollars     (well over its estimated eight to twelve)
        thus a daughter of one of the very few native Irish houses
        provenance by descent to the late owner & she's in red
        with a translucent veil on the back of her head      bride-like
            was the daughter of                & married firstly
            & had four sons       & when her husband died on active
            service she married  & later at his death   married another
she cannot be too much guarded in her behaviour
or gone apple-stealing under the sea


coda : listening to a radio show about earth's twin planet & looking at lady
mary boyle nursing her son three hundred years ago while nursing my toddler while she
puts matchbox cars in my pockets & wondering why write poems at all—


        • *Portrait of Lady Mary Boyle and her son Charles,* Studio of Sir Godfrey Kneller, c. 1700

self-portrait, seated

her I have painted
myself painting myself    *her aged* 20 her & the mess of the body her
palette hooked on her thumb her five
brushes her like seven fingers    her eyes seem outsized or her head or
it's her body as background that makes it seem so                her series of women against
dark or neutral with hands folded her    which cease after 1554 so
it is assumed (with depressing
predictability)    that she made no art after her marrying          (with her sister
one face)                the way the two could fold & close like
                    her a diptych    showing herself themselves making art
(music being art)    her I like how you're looking at me except
you're not her looking at me but rather at an idea of yourself in her reverse
her steady & studious    her serious & a little tired around the eyes    her holding still
        (quiet   ) hands folded    her it occurs
to me that I've never seen anyone paint in person & so
my images of what her it must be like are romantic & static & her silent & never boring

• Caterina van Hemessen, *Self Portrait Seated at an Easel,* 1548

self-portrait, for new year's day


some things women do with their hands
                    disappear her own hands
her face her blurred      turning toward forward or
away her          ironing board her level her shop-vac
        (see also                    *netherlandish*    *flemish*    *quiet*
only low
        countries          south
                    philadelphia) her          sea
                                    level or below
her blurred turning her three
foot level her aged thirty-seven her cordless drill
her tool bucket one of those plastic tubs reused one
of her   reduce reuse
        those plastic buckets with the awful
graphic of a baby tipping headfirst into under
the graphic for no or      graphic circle slash or    the no symbol


                    • Kate Kern Mundie, *Self-portrait with Tools and Ironing Board (age 37)*, 2011

children, pears, wet nurse


also        a pear-shaped jug in the farthest narrative fragment
foregrounded her decorative
smallish & whitest breasts        her unused        the wet nurse & her
globular useful  the baby swaddled & stiff as though
strapped to a board                (is that baby strapped to a board)
if the toddler interrupts her bath for some fruit
if the wet nurse looks suspicious & perhaps looks
about to discipline        (don't touch that fruit)   she's the same
if        when they are dressed in a less famous
similar image    the same wet nurse        the same expression
a smaller baby            if when they are dressed they are not left-handed
if when we wean will I
care less about breasts     it becomes you     my
sister     I think so hard so that the milk won't come                the milk comes

• Ecole française, *Gabrielle d'Estrées au bain*, circa 1598-99
• Fontainebleau School, *Portrait présumé de Gabrielle d'Estrées et de sa soeur la duchesse de Villars*, circa 1594
• Fontainebleau School, *Gabrielle d'Estrées and her sister, the Duchess of Villars*, circa 1590s

the children are not word-final schwas
if        when    they are
similar images   (if when we)
hissing like her
skirt her shells her book in good light (the *g*
          is silent          he says) I sink
&               liminal domestic    the representation
of ephemera    (the milk
the apple)                        the representation
of ephemera (how she wears her title     translucent
& half-length)          one face the way
we could click shut for travel
          it becomes you it
          becomes you it becomes
          you it becomes

the listening girl (repetitions exist)


yourself in chapters simultaneously
so that we are between    entr'acted        mezzanined
everything is warmer in oranges & leaded glass light (the *g*
          is silent          he tells me)        the gesture which
could be read    I suppose        as a *shush* looks
more like coyness                    the original sense
          was quiet still        an invitation to witness
a rope for a handrail        a third person in their lamplight
a foot from beneath her skirts & a hand working
their bodies their clothes their shift        managing light how to
efficiently run a household        how to        surprise
me (I hide        she says)        the gesture which silences
has classical origins but  *shush*        a repetition of *sh sh*
          (let's have a bit of shush) husht husht yourself    I hide

• Nicolas Maes, *The Listening Housewife (The Eavesdropper)*, 1656
• Nicolas Maes, *The Listening Housewife*, 1655

the listening girl (repetitions exist)


yourself mezzanined     warmer   efficient shift
a hand working     a foot working     let's have
a bit of *shush*     between above & below stairs
            in a conspiracy we breathe together

the language of gestures          he liked making
paintings of women spinning    reading    cooking
lacemaking        listen in listen listen hush
            you're making so much noise I can't hear you

let us consider the surface of domestic order
or not    let us consider the domestic
            or feral pigeon let us pluck it like a chicken
let us empty the wine jug let us be reckless & overheard

this image lets us be privy to      above & below
stairs     different privities    defense of domestic territories

• Nicolas Maes, *The Listening Housewife (The Eavesdropper)*, 1656
• Nicolas Maes, *The Listening Housewife*, 1655

woman plucking a duck


a gun a collander & someone in the next room
& a wineglass in the next room & windows & doors
make for simultaneous spaces & I've never seen
anyone so casual about apples
                                pouring forth     the basket
gives way to flat surface     two dead
ducks & one alive cat plus
a possible breeze on her neck     equals
something domestic (a still life) & arranged to be so
        (she has the duck in a kind of modified football hold)
so interior        housewifery clutter & if the cat
already caused disarray     she doesn't care
the duck on the floor & the duck on her lap
before & after            roasted with said apples


• Nicolas Maes, *Woman Plucking a Duck*, 1656

& child, with apple tree & bread & doll


the representation of ephemera          the apple the crust
of bread          this is me
                 this is my
                 this is mine
she wears her drapery & not housewifely          very secular
fashion   the narrow sexy corners of her eyes      sometimes
toddlers subsist entirely on baguette ends     I've been trying to do
my hair that way all morning     with bareass baby in an orchard
          thick with underbrush   furrowed with worry     a choking hazard
in his charity she's
naked & nursing a baby with older toddlers either
hanging around her neck or touching her thigh keeping
their claims on access to her body                (narrow-waisted
                                                   high-breasted)


one two three apples above their heads   a little girl with a saxon princess
doll practices   charity   is a woman with children from the 14th century onwards

• Lucas Cranach the Elder, *The Virgin & Child Under an Apple Tree*, 1530
• Lucas Cranach the Elder, *Charity*, 1537-50; *Charity*, 1534

a woman scraping parsnips, with a child standing by


bring the knife toward the body toward the body
watch now watch me bring the knife toward
plane the woody surface a sharp parallel knife
keywords        food people vegetables child woman young
vegetable kid person adult female lady two people two
two two persons indoor domestic scene scenes homely inside
indoors interior interiors vertical preparing sitting sit sits seated
domestic parsnips parsnip scraping basket knife house home
tags    woman child cap basket knife jug skirt apron ewer bodice some things
women do with their hands working by a window
the girl is beautifully grumpy & learning something
          boil the parsnips until tender
          boil the eggs very hard
& within the limits of browns & reds & greens they
disappear into their domestic & the representation of work
not hardship & *hardship* has been related to labor since 14th c.
English is a daughter language & there's nothing
odd about that
                    we'll make a stew we'll make saltfish & fix
                    our parsnips lenten
in the north of Ireland they brewed parsnips with malt
for a pleasant peasant beer        but I doubt it stick a spoon
upright in it & sweet jesus watch your fingers


• Nicholas Maes, *A Woman Scraping Parsnips, with a Child Standing by Her,* 1655 woman & child in a pantry


a small room under stairs          (at least
there's a window) & there's a window through
the doorway & it's open          it's giving
way to light & breezes   a breeze of air in my hair
you said                              from bread
late Latin bread     paradise is the pantry
a covey of bread & pastry & all crockery
one-point perspective of the checkerboard
floor               two *throughviews*               you
create space by showing the light outside it
it's a view in & a view out          we call that domestic
the boy is in a jerkin     which has straps to check him
keep him out of traffic & the like          a beautiful
long-haired boy          every day is like Sunday


• Pieter de Hooch, *Woman with a Child in a Pantry*, c. 1655-60.

a coherent interior


a continuous landscape available through clear glass
painted over      later      a continuous interior
maintained by her dress            the left logically
related to the right        a tiny perfect apple
passes from her left hand to his right      a choking hazard
(some things women do with their hands)
            queen mirror    torso textured    as in *woven*
            the surface sounds        splitting up the middle


a convex mirror shows us how the space is closed        see *flemish*
            & see also                                    *quiet*
the perspective disappears into the farthest
narrative point & they are busy keeping both
the landscape & the interior inside their eyes
                is anybody going to eat that apple

• Hans Memling, *The van Nieuwenhove Diptych,* 1487
• Jay DeFeo, *The Annunciation,* 1957-59

family, with apples


the two bad apples are a premonition
lot 36    it sold   (a jewel) *her apple &*
                                *her father* but the important
thing about an apple     (in his left hand   firmly gripped)
but the important thing about an apple
like many other things we do not understand
thence by descent to the present
but the important thing about an apple
how it here replaces an orb        that is
something regal something celestial & what
is orbed in his left hand is something
everyday something Sunday something interior

when are you going to stop kissing him on the lips
a neighbor asked        he's such a big boy now

• Gerard David, *The Holy Family,* c. 1460 - 1523.
• George Oppen, "From a Photograph," 1962.
• Margaret Wise Brown, *The Important Book,* 1949.

woman with teething


we know her by habit & attitude & position
she is unmarked & in the dark with only the child
small format    closed   a density without openings
faces touching      because he has kept
her awake    she is softer through
the varnish      nearly monochromatic almost as though
her hands come out of nowhere          his swaddle obviously a shroud
          (an early sense of the verb    related to *shred*      was to cover
so as to protect)

the person who wrote *the Child gives vent to his joyous*
*activity by his movements & by shouting or singing*
          has never held a teething child overnight
simultaneous eruption of his upper central incisors
his coral bracelet both amulet & chewtoy        he must have
looked in the mirror      her hands come out of the dark
it's me   I've got you now                I've got you

• Andrea Mantegna, *Madonna Poldi Pezzoli (The Sleeping Child)*, c. 1490.
• Andrea Mantegna, *Madonna & Child* (Bergamo), c. 1480.
• Paul Kristeller, *Andrea Mantegna,* 1901.

the good mother does not say 'my child do you want?'

we are warmer     before & after
my hair thick with worry
a sidelong waterview *shush*
          gestures exist     shift     I'm making so much
noise you can't look me in the eye behavior is
communication          it gets in everything
two people seated     two people cooking     two people
reading          two people interior     two people
sound     with no object          see listen
see also Jan Steen's *Mother & Child* in which
the distinction between hausfrau
          & virgin dissappears
virgin & baby-led weaning
that apple          looks like it's had a fall from a table
a bruise     a dent                    open wide
when someone offers you pap or else
later you will receive nothing netherlandish
virgin with spoon
          there are many variations
          extant     intended
          for private devotion          with milk soup

          • Gerard David, *Virgin & Child with the Milk Soup* [four versions], c. 1510-20

· 65 ·

the good mother does not say 'my child do you want?'


the nursing child is a passive rückenfigur
by contrast        & view into another room or
windowscape      in which her gesture is unintelligible
in which sometimes a pacifier is just a pacifier
figures take up or define space    sometimes a dog
          our lady of the mush
          virgin & child with rosary as chewelry
& wooden spoon & wooden spoon & cherry branch
          (he is about to eat a leaf      holy face
                              cut from a book
long ago) book open domestic hours
he married a miniaturist         his wife was a miniaturist
rest on the flight into egret   [sic] [stet]  rest rest
a market-tested secular representation    indeed  a bestseller
connect-the-dots         & there was never an original


• Gerard David, *Virgin & Child with the Milk Soup* [four versions], c. 1510-20

the good mother does not say 'my child do you want?'


while I was distracted his shift slipped
off & nothing else changed & no one noticed
without the use of X-radiograph his shift
dress disappears & we can reasonably assume
this was not the first in an intended series
milk soup thick with worry      I add too much
milk goodnight mush
          I like how her hands never change some
          things women do with them his legs
          kick squirm the same way a pattern
          followed      hold this spoon while
I put this other spoon in your mouth distract
you with spoons with a branch of cherries with singing
the lonely goatherd      subsequent copies with fewer
flowers & a basket holding correspondence before
& after genres exist shift      a book tells me
cherries bread & knife are domestic symbols of the good life
                    (none where none)
two interior people      choose a moment & mark it


• Gerard David, *Virgin & Child with the Milk Soup* [four versions], c. 1510-20

supermatka (one)


I could be supermatka    in the right
ikea lighting    virgin & child in kitchen        *home game* literally
*laundry    wash*        *cooking*    labelled for ease of use
virgin & child    labelled for ease        with orange segment    from *super*
            above & beyond        the virgin de la leche tandem
            nurses a toddler & Bernard of Clairvaux
            goes    above & beyond the call    I think
            we can all agree on that        Bernard's
            little red feet peek out from under
            their shimmering cloak of miraculous
            lactaction        her feet on winged
            floating heads    like the hands in Fra Angelico's
            San Marco mockery (cell 7)        I cannot be supermatka if my children
                            won't put on their jackets & hats


• Elźbieta Jabłońska, *Supermatka*, 2002.
• Unknown artist (Peru), *Virgin de la Leche with Christ Child & St. Bernard Clarivaux,* 1680.
• Fra Angelico, *Mockery of Christ,* 1441.

supermatka (two)

I could be supermatka    & assume a masculine
position    triangular    pyramidal    the good mother
                                the matka-polka
                                the satiated baby
                                the male artist (cf. van der weyden et al)
                        I was thinking first of Luke drawing the virgin & child
but the Durán madonna instead  the red red red  the boy on one knee
        he (restless realistic) crumples the pages
(she doesn't care)        has beautiful sweet feet  the red triangle of her in a niche
        supermatka doesn't care about the domestic artifacts & bits
collecting in stacks    leaning & curling    unfinished pine    tulips    boombox
his bare feet      on her one knee      I love you kiss sit still
he is realistic  leaning & curling  her hands (some things
women do with their hands)  hold him steady
I could be supermatka with my boots    on

                        *at my feet there is nothing. I am absolved*
                        *of history.*

                        • Elżbieta Jabłońska, *Supermatka*, 2002.
                        • Rogier van der Weyden, *Durán Madonna*, c. 1435-38.
                        • Elizabeth Robinson, "Mary & No Savior," 2008.

supermatka (three)


I could be supermatka    via google streetview
too many shoes
too many shoes untied laces
I go in to straighten their blankets        to straighten them their heads
hanging off the beds      & I'd give anything to sleep        for fifteen minutes
like Asher sleeps        arms thrown open over
his head sweet        smell the whole
room full of his breathing        I don't know much at all
about the mythologies & iconographies of superheroes
          he falls asleep in the car I carry him up from the street
          his fuzzy slippers his forty pounds of sleep asleep
virgin & child in mudroom virgin & child in foyer
                              from *focus* domestic hearth
    she says maybe   the iphone is the convex mirror of our time


• Elżbieta Jabłońska, *Supermatka*, 2002.

# notes & sources :

x y z & & :

I. 1 - 2. Gertrude Stein, "Patriarchal Poetry."
11. Gail Griffin, "Oval."
13 - 14. Louis Zukofsky, "A Song for the Year's End."
II. 1 - 3. Kenneth Goldsmith, *The Weather*.
6 - 7. Mina Loy, "Parturition."
14. Julie Carr, *100 Notes on Violence*.
III. 1 - 2. Maxine Chernoff, "Have You a Daughter?"
14. Rachel Blau DuPlessis, "Draft 2: SHE."
IV. 1. James Joyce, *Finnegans Wake*. [3:14 559.33]
14. Jen Currin, "A Patriot." *The Inquisition Yours*.
V. 6 - 7. Samuel Richardson, *Clarissa*. II. xxxiii. 227 (OED)
9 - 11. Online Etymology Dictionary
13 - 14. Elizabeth Willis, "The Witch." *Address*.
VI. 1. Kate Kern Mundie.
14. Karen Weiser, in email.
VII. 14. Ernest Hemingway, "Hills Like White Elephants."
IX. 13 - 14. Elizabeth Robinson, "The Hinge Trees."
X. *for Cleo Miller*.
1. Gertrude Stein, "Patriarchal Poetry."
14. Sarah Campbell, *Everything We Could Ask For*.
XI. 1 - 2. Lyn Hejinian, "Eleven Eyes."
12 - 13. Susan Howe, *Hinge Picture*.
13 - 14. Eric Keenaghan, "Openings: Some Notes on the Political in Rachel Blau DuPlessis' *Drafts*."
XII. 1. Peter Gizzi, *Threshold Songs*.

5 - 8. US Social Security Administration. List of most popular baby names
 since 1880. http://www.ssa.gov/oact/babynames/

13 - 14. Bernadette Mayer, "Eve of Easter."

XIII. 1. Gertrude Stein, *The Autobiography of Alice B. Toklas.*

13 - 14. Henry James, in a letter.

XIV. 1. Stan Mir, "Night."

14. Andrew Zawacki, "Limit Sonnet."

XV. 1. William Butler Yeats, "Among School Children"

8 - 11. "hex," OED etym. (*Word Study* 1968)

14. Laura Walker, *Swarm Lure.*

XVI. 1 - 2. Matvei Yankelevich, "Next Summer," *Alpha Donut.*

14. Lorine Niedecker, "Next Year, or I fly my rounds, Tempestuous."

XVII. 1 - 3. Bhanu Kapil, "Some Autobiographical Information about Cyborgs,"
 *Incubation: A Space for Monsters.*

XIX. 2 - 4. Judith Newman, "The Consequences of Motherhood" [review
 of Anne Enright's *Making Babies*]. *New York Times,* 11 May 2012.

13 - 14. Paul LaFarge, *Haussmann, or the Distinction.*

XX. *for Aki Mir*

1. Stan Mir, "Night."

13 - 14. Carolina Maugeri, "A Note on School of the Holy Beast."

XXI. 1 - 2. Joseph McElroy, "Night Soul"

5 - 9. Rosemarie Sokol Chang & Nicholas S. Thompson, "Whines, Cries,
 and Motherese: Their Relative Power to Distract." *Journal of Social,
 Evolutionary, & Cultural Psychology* 2011, 5(2).

14. Radiohead. "Karma Police."

XXII. 1 - 2. Eugene Guillevic, "Acute Angle" from *Geometries.*

14. Dan Featherston, "Goat."

XXIII. 1 - 2. Rosmarie Waldrop. "Any Single Thing." *Plume.*
 http://plumepoetry.com/?page_id=1031

XXIV. 1. Deleuze & Guattari, *A Thousand Plateaus*.

2 - 9. *OED* ("girl").

10. Ariana Reines, trans. *Preliminary Materials for a Theory of the Young-Girl (Triple Canopy)*.

XXV. 1. Jen Coleman, "Psalm for Dogs and Sorcerers."

13 - 14. Brian Teare, "Embodiment (White Birch)."

XXVI. 1. Stacy Doris, *Knot*.

2. Virginia Woolf, "Kew Gardens."

13 - 14. Walt Whitman, *Leaves of Grass*.

XXVII. 13 - 14. Edmund B. Wilson, *The Cell in Development & Inheritance* (1900). [Three births in forty-two lines.]

XXVIII. 1 - 2. William Carlos Williams, "Children's Games" from *Pictures from Brueghel*.

XXIX. 1. T.S. Eliot, "Ash-Wednesday."

14. Rachel Blau DuPlessis, "Draft 2: SHE."

XXX. 13 - 14. Laura Spagnoli, "Letters to My Niece," *My Dazzledent Days*.

November 2010 - March 2013.


notes for clothespin :

after Claes Oldenberg's Clothespin, at 1500 Market St., Philadelphia.

This poem was commissioned for *Sound Sculptures,* a series of sonic responses to various sculptures commissioned by the Philadelphia Redevelopment Authority's Percent for Art program. *Sound Sculptures* was commissioned by the Philadelphia Redevelopment Authority and was curated and produced by Bowerbird. www.phillysoundsculptures.com

September 2012.

genre scenes :

Ainsworth, Maryan. *Gerard David: A Purity of Vision in an Age of Transition.*

Durantini, Mary Frances. *The Child in Seventeenth-Century Dutch Painting.*

Sutton, Peter C., ed. *Masters of Seventeenth Century Dutch Genre Painting.* Philadelphia: Philadelphia Museum of Art and U Pennsylvania P, 1984.

Wolf, Bryan Jay. *Vermeer.* Chicago: U Chicago P, 2001.

October 2012 - June 2013

PHOTO: COLIN LENTON

PATTIE MCCARTHY is the author of four previous collections from Apogee Press: *Marybones, Table Alphabetical of Hard Words, Verso,* and *bk of (h)rs,* as well as *Nulls* (horse less press). She is also the author of over a dozen chapbooks, including *margerykempething, scenes from the lives of my parents,* and *worrywort* (a collaboration with Jenn McCreary). She was awarded a Pew Fellowship in the Arts in 2011. In August 2013, McCarthy was an artist resident at the Elizabeth Bishop House in Great Village, Nova Scotia. She teaches at Temple University.

## OTHER POETRY TITLES
## FROM APOGEE PRESS

**MAXINE CHERNOFF**

*Among the Names*
*The Turning*

**VALERIE COULTON**

*The Cellar Dreamer*
*open book*
*passing world pictures*

**TSERING WANGMO DHOMPA**

*In the Absent Everyday*
*My rice tastes like the lake*
*Rules of the House*

**KATHLEEN FRASER**

*Discrete Categories Forced into Coupling*

**PAUL HOOVER**

*Edge and Fold*

**ALICE JONES**

*Gorgeous Mourning*
*Plunge*

**STEFANIE MARLIS**

*cloudlife*
*fine*

**A MAXWELL**

*Peeping Mot*

**EDWARD KLEINSCHMIDT MAYES**
*Speed of Life*

**PATTIE MCCARTHY**

*bk of (h)rs*
*marybones*
*Table Alphabetical of Hard Words*
*Verso*

**DENISE NEWMAN**

*Human Forest*
*Wild Goods*

**ELIZABETH ROBINSON**

*Also Known As*
*Apostrophe*
*Apprehend*

**EDWARD SMALLFIELD**

*equinox*
*The Pleasures of C*

**COLE SWENSEN**

*Oh*

**BARBARA TOMASH**

*Arboreal*

**TRUONG TRAN**

*dust and conscience*
*four letter words*
*placing the accents*
*within the margin*

**LAURA WALKER**

*Follow-Haswed*

**KHATY XIONG**

*Poor Anima*

**TO ORDER OR FOR MORE
INFORMATION GO TO
WWW.APOGEEPRESS.COM**